NEW BOOKS FOR NEW READERS

Phyllis MacAdam, *General Editor*

Into the Wilderness

The Lewis and Clark Expedition

James J. Holmberg

THE UNIVERSITY PRESS OF KENTUCKY

Publication of this volume was made possible by
The Kentucky Humanities Council, Inc.

Scholarly publisher for the Commonwealth,
serving Bellarmine University, Berea College, Centre
College of Kentucky, Eastern Kentucky University,
The Filson Historical Society, Georgetown College,
Kentucky Historical Society, Kentucky State University,
Morehead State University, Murray State University,
Northern Kentucky University, Transylvania University,
University of Kentucky, University of Louisville,
and Western Kentucky University.

Editorial and Sales Offices: The University Press of Kentucky
663 South Limestone Street, Lexington, Kentucky 40508-4008

07 06 05 04   5 4 3 2

Library of Congress Cataloging-in-Publication Data

Holmberg, James J. (James John), 1958-
 Into the wilderness : the Lewis and Clark Expedition / James J.
Holmberg.
    p. cm. — (New books for new readers)
  ISBN 0-8131-0913-2 (pbk. : alk. paper)
  1. Lewis and Clark Expedition (1804-1806) 2. West (U.S.)—Discovery
and exploration. 3. West (U.S.)—Description and travel. 4. Readers
for new literates. I. Title. II. Series.
  F592.7.H73 2003
  917.804'2—dc21

                    2003012047

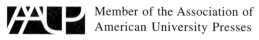

Contents

Foreword

This book is published as Kentucky joins the rest of the country in commemorating the bicentennial of the Lewis and Clark Expedition to the Pacific Ocean, an astonishing journey that shaped our nation. This tale is a Kentucky story as well, for Kentucky *was* the West in 1800, and the brave Kentuckians who made the journey comprised nearly half of the men in the Corps of Discovery.

The Kentucky Humanities Council began New Books for New Readers because Kentucky's adult literacy students want books that recognize their intelligence and experience while meeting their need for simplicity in writing. The first twelve titles in the New Books for New Readers series have helped many adult students open the window on the wonderful world of literacy. At the same time, these New Books, with their plain language and compelling stories of Kentucky history and culture, have found a wider audience among accomplished readers of all ages who recognize a good story when they see one.

As we publish this thirteenth book in the series, we thank our authors and our readers, who together have proved that New Books and the humanities are for everyone. Through your efforts, we too, in the words of William Clark, will "proceed on."

This volume was made possible by contributions from the Kentucky Humanities Council's Board of Directors and from many individuals all across the Commonwealth who financially support our mission. We especially recognize Martin F. Schmidt, who has steadfastly believed in this ongoing project.

We are grateful for the advice, support, and long partnership provided to us by the University of Kentucky and the University Press of Kentucky. The Council thanks all of our friends who share our commitment to the important role that reading books plays in the lives of the people of our Commonwealth. Homes without books are lives without hope.

Virginia G. Smith, Executive Director
Kentucky Humanities Council, Inc.

TELLING **KENTUCKY'S** STORY

Acknowledgments

It was my pleasure to work with a number of people and institutions in writing *Into the Wilderness*. It is a better book because of their assistance and I thank them. This book never would have come about without the vision of Kentucky Humanities Council Executive Director Virginia Smith. She saw the opportunity to inform an important audience about the Lewis and Clark Expedition and Kentucky's connection to it and recruited me to write about the adventure. Series editor Dr. Phyllis MacAdam was a pleasure to work with. Her editorial expertise and suggestions were invaluable.

The focus group, composed of students in the adult literacy and English as a Second Language programs at Ahrens Adult Education Center in Louisville, was a pleasure to work with. Led by instructors Diane Graybill and Peggy Bradley, the students read and discussed each chapter. They offered suggestions and asked questions. Our meetings often ranged over a variety of Lewis and Clark topics and extended to other aspects of American history. My thanks to Sharon Parker, Troy Thomas, LaShirl Reed, Melissa Robinson, Carla Robinson, Shirley Evans, Fred Hollis, Terri Murrell, Tina Coffey, James Hinkle, Charlene Martin, Timothy Pound, Kathryn Ross, Carrie Thomas, Demetrius Banks, Shatara Hargrove, Troy Ritchie, Jeffrey Belton, John Bube Jr., Kita Compton, Akbar Adeibparvar, Freda Austin, Kenneth Banks, Nerlande Tisoit, Guixia Wang, Tanita Wright, Jeff Zeng, and Lan Nhon. Another reviewer was my daughter, Emily Holmberg, and I thank her.

Thanks to The Filson Historical Society for providing many of the illustrations, and special thanks to Jennifer Cole and Rebecca Rice of The Filson for their assistance. My appreciation to Virginia Smith for the work she put into her sketches. Joslyn Art Museum in Omaha, Nebraska, allowed us to reproduce the Bodmer engraving. Thanks to the Clymer Museum of Art for the cover illustration, "Lewis and Clark in the Bitterroots" by John F. Clymer, 1967. Thank you to Ed Hamilton for the image of his York statue. The Independence National Historical Park and the Lewis and Clark Trail Heritage Foundation were, as ever, cooperative and a pleasure to work with.

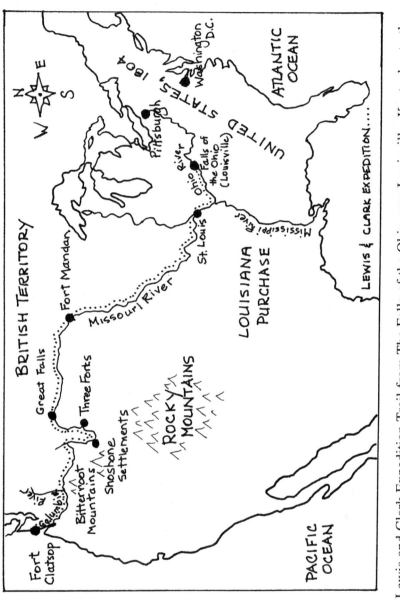

Lewis and Clark Expedition Trail from The Falls of the Ohio near Louisville, Kentucky, to the Pacific Ocean (1803-1805).

Introduction

Two hundred years ago the United States was a young nation. Its western border was the Mississippi River. Most Americans lived east of the Appalachian Mountains. The country west of the Mississippi was a mystery. What was out there? What was beyond their cities, towns, and farms?

In 1803 President Thomas Jefferson decided to find out. He sent the first official United States exploring party into this mysterious West. The group was named the Corps of Discovery. Its leaders were Meriwether Lewis and William Clark. President Jefferson wanted them to find a route across western North America all the way to the Pacific Ocean. Along the way they were ordered to explore the country, taking notes and collecting samples of plants, animals, and Indian life as they went.

Before they left, there was much planning and preparing to do. They selected 30 brave men to join them. The party included people of different cultures and different races. Most were white men, but one black man went on the trip. Several men were part American Indian. Half of the men were from Kentucky or had ties to Kentucky. During the expedition a young Indian woman and her baby joined the explorers. Lewis's large dog, Seaman, went on the journey. The group had to have the help of the Indians to succeed. Without their help, the explorers never would have reached the Pacific or returned safely.

The explorers traveled some eight thousand miles west of

the Mississippi in about two and a half years. They worked their way up the Missouri River, across the Rocky Mountains, down the Columbia River to the Pacific, and back home again. Along the way they had many adventures, suffered hardships, and faced death. Sometimes they were hungry, and sometimes they were in great danger. But they had good times, too. The explorers were like a big family. They had to work together to succeed.

The Lewis and Clark Expedition began in 1803 and ended in 1806. It is the greatest exploring venture in the history of the United States. Lewis and Clark became American heroes 200 years ago, and they are still American heroes today.

This is the story of the Lewis and Clark Expedition.

1

Thomas Jefferson's Dream

Thomas Jefferson had a dream. As a boy in the 1750s, he lived with his family near the Blue Ridge Mountains of Virginia. At the time, that was as far west as most American colonists lived. Beyond lay an unknown land. He wondered what the land to the west was like.

Sometimes men crossed the mountains to hunt. When they came back, they told stories of the land beyond the mountains. They talked about a rich, beautiful land called Kentucky and about the wide Ohio River that flowed toward the setting sun. Young Tom also heard stories about what might lay beyond the mighty Mississippi River. Did giant animals still roam that country? Were there mountains of salt? Tom listened and wanted to know more about this land. He decided that one day he would find out. But until that day, he would dream of what might be beyond the Blue Ridge Mountains and the Mississippi River.

As he grew older, Thomas Jefferson never forgot this dream. He read about western travelers and their trips. By writing letters and talking with some of these men he learned more. Tom collected fossils, Indian artifacts, and other samples they brought back and asked them to bring him more, so he could learn about the plants, animals, and people that lived in the West. He wanted to know everything he could about this mysterious land.

Events in Tom's life and in America kept him from pursuing his dream for some time. He married and had a family. He made his living as a lawyer and a farmer. Virginia needed leaders, and Tom served in its government. In the 1770s leaders in the American Colonies began to talk about independence from England. Tom Jefferson went to Philadelphia to meet with other patriots. In 1776 he wrote the most famous document in American history, the Declaration of Independence, announcing the birth of a new nation. The Revolutionary War would decide if there would be a United States of America. This was not a good time to learn more about the West.

In 1783 the Revolutionary War ended. America had won its independence. Thomas Jefferson was very busy as one of the leaders of the new country, but he could also think about exploring again. The United States lay east of the Mississippi. The land west of the Mississippi was not part of the new nation. This fact did not bother Jefferson. He still wanted to send an American explorer into the mysterious West, all the way to the Pacific Ocean.

Over the next ten years, Jefferson tried three times to send explorers into the West, but each try failed. The first man Jefferson asked was his friend George Rogers Clark, a war hero from Kentucky. Clark was busy defending Kentucky from Indian attacks and had money and legal problems caused by the war. He turned Jefferson down. Little did either man know that 20 years later Clark's youngest brother, William, would help lead the expedition that fulfilled Jefferson's dream.

A few years later, Jefferson met an American in France and

Thomas Jefferson (The Filson Historical Society)

got him to try to explore the American West in an unusual way. Instead of leaving from Kentucky and going west, this man tried to reach the West by going east across Russia and then crossing the Pacific to get there. He was arrested in Russia and sent back to France.

In 1793 Jefferson tried again. This time the explorer was a French scientist visiting America. He was going to leave from Kentucky, but he got involved with French spies and never went west.

Three times Thomas Jefferson had tried to get someone to go on a western expedition, and three times the attempt had failed. He must have wondered if his dream would ever come true. Ten years passed, and in 1803 Jefferson finally had the pleasure of seeing his long dreamed of expedition take shape and begin its journey to the Pacific.

In 1801 Jefferson became president of the United States. The duties of his job kept him busy, and he didn't try to send explorers out west right away. But in 1802 he read something that made him decide that America had to send explorers to the Pacific. The reason was his fear of the British and their plans for North America. Jefferson read about the travels of a Scotsman named Alexander Mackenzie. In 1793 Mackenzie had reached the Pacific by traveling across Canada. He wrote a book about his journey. In it he said that the British should control the Pacific Northwest and keep others out. This scared Jefferson. He believed the United States couldn't let that happen. As president he could send American explorers to the West. Not only would they strengthen America's claim to the Pacific Northwest, but they could also collect samples and write about the country, something he had wanted for many years. Jefferson began planning for a U.S. government expedition whose members would be soldiers.

Jefferson had seen three attempts fail. This time, everything must be done right. The right leader must be chosen. The right training must be done. The right men must be picked, and the right planning must be carried out. Mistakes in these important areas might doom the expedition.

Who could he ask to be the leader? It had to be a military man who was young and fit. The man also had to be smart enough to carry out all the expedition's planning and work. The leader would have to keep records about the land, the plants, the animals, and the peoples of the West. Thomas Jefferson also had to trust him.

Jefferson chose a young army officer named Meriwether Lewis. Lewis was born in Virginia in 1774. The Lewis and Jefferson families were neighbors. Lewis was a young boy when his father died. As he grew older, Meriwether helped run the family farm. He also went to school, roamed the woods, hunted, and learned about healing plants from his mother. As the years passed, he grew into a tall, dark-haired, handsome young man. He liked adventure and longed for a chance to travel west.

In 1795 Lewis joined the army as an officer. He was sent west to Ohio. For a short time, he served under William Clark. Clark, a tall, red-headed Kentuckian, was a natural leader. The two men liked each other and became friends. After Clark left the army in 1796 and returned home to Louisville, Kentucky, they kept in touch. Lewis stayed in the army and traveled around the western United States—to Kentucky, Tennessee, Indiana, Ohio, and Michigan—learning about the people, their politics, and the land.

In February 1801 President Jefferson asked Lewis to be his private secretary. The young officer would answer Jefferson's questions about the western U.S., write reports, and do other work for him. Lewis jumped at the chance. Working for the president was much better than the life of a soldier on the frontier. Jefferson liked this talented young man and trusted him. When Jefferson decided to send an expedition to the Pacific, he knew Lewis was just the man for the job.

Meriwether Lewis by Charles Wilson Peale (Independence National Historical Park, Philadelphia, Pennsylvania)

Time was important. Jefferson and Lewis set about preparing for the trip. The president took care of paperwork and got $2,500 from Congress for the expedition. He taught Lewis about plants and animals and other subjects. He even sent him to Pennsylvania to study science and medicine from the best men in their fields. Lewis bought supplies needed for the trip. He got medicine, tools, guns, uniforms, scientific equipment, food, Indian trade goods, and more. Much more than $2,500 was spent, but Lewis got what was needed, and Jefferson made sure the bills were paid.

Making friends with the Indians would be very important.

Lewis was supposed to tell these tribes that they were now the children of the "Great White Father" (the President). A good way to make friends with the Indians was to give them gifts. Lewis bought little mirrors, fishhooks, coats, American flags, colorful handkerchiefs, blankets, tobacco, and beads. Not only could these items be used as gifts, but they could also be traded for things the expedition needed.

Before Lewis left Washington, he had one more task, a very important one. Lewis and Jefferson decided that they needed another army officer on the trip. Not only could he help Lewis, but if Lewis got sick, or was hurt, or died, the other officer could take over. Lewis wanted his friend and former commander, William Clark, to go. Jefferson agreed. The young explorer knew he needed someone with Clark's experience and ability to help the expedition succeed. Lewis believed that Clark should be equal to him in every way. On June 19, 1803, he wrote his friend a letter inviting him to join the expedition as its co-leader. He mailed it and got ready to leave Washington.

On July 5, 1803, Meriwether Lewis set out on his famous journey. The young explorer had done everything he could in the East. The West and its wonders—and dangers—awaited him. Thomas Jefferson's dream just might come true this time.

2

Down the Ohio

While his letter to William Clark made its way west toward The Falls of the Ohio, Meriwether Lewis headed to Pittsburgh. The weather was warm and dry, and the young explorer made good time on the dusty roads. On the afternoon of July 15, Lewis rode into Pittsburgh.

He had ordered a keelboat built for the expedition. This would be the expedition's main boat all the way to the upper Missouri River. It was 55 feet long, with a sail and oars. Upon checking, he learned it wasn't ready. Day after day the young captain urged the boat builder and his workers to work harder, but it did no good. The builder kept promising it would be ready soon, but six weeks passed before he finally finished it. Lewis was very angry and wrote the president that the boat builder was always "either drunk or sick."

Lewis was so eager to leave that he left the day his boat was done. On August 31, he set out down the Ohio River. With him were crews for the keelboat and a second, smaller boat called a pirogue, which helped carry supplies. Also with him were his faithful Newfoundland breed dog, Seaman, and some young men who wanted to join the expedition.

The little band's progress was slow. By late summer of 1803, the water level in the Ohio was lower than anyone could remember. In fact, it was so low in some places that Lewis had to hire horses and oxen from nearby farms to drag the boat downstream. He also had to have his men pull the boat over sand bars. His smaller boat leaked. While they were stopped at Wheeling, West Virginia, he bought a red pirogue to carry more supplies. He reached Cincinnati on September 28. About a week later he collected bones of prehistoric animals at Big Bone Lick in Kentucky. They were for President Jefferson, but an accident kept them from reaching him. Slowly, day by day, the keelboat moved downstream toward The Falls of the Ohio and Louisville, where William Clark waited.

The Falls of the Ohio was a series of rapids on the river. It was here that Louisville, Clarksville, and other towns had been founded. Clark had moved across the river to Clarksville, Indiana Territory, earlier that year. He had sold his farm outside Louisville to his brother Jonathan. He had called the place home since moving to Kentucky as a fourteen-year-old boy in 1785. William had spent years trying to help his brother George with his legal and money troubles. As a result he had put himself deeply in debt. To try to recover, he sold the farm. He and George settled on a farm at Clarksville, named in the old hero's honor. It would be here, at The Falls of the Ohio, that important expedition events would take place.

Lewis's letter reached Clark on July 17. His invitation asking Clark to join him in the "dangers and honors" of the expedition arrived at a good time. William Clark was looking for a new start. Not only was the proposed trip to the Pacific an exciting adventure, but if they succeeded, Clark knew they would be rewarded. This trip might be just the new start he was looking for. The Kentuckian wasted no time in answering his friend's letter. Writing Lewis on July 18, he said he would

William Clark by Joseph Bush (The Filson Historical Society)

"cheerfully join" him. He wrote about the good timing, the possible rewards, and his eagerness to undertake such a dangerous mission with his friend. He also promised that he would do as his friend asked and find young men who were the best hunters and woodsmen in the Louisville area for their "Corps of Discovery."

While Lewis waited for the boat to be finished and then made his way down the Ohio, Clark was busy getting ready for his partner's arrival. He spent most of his time in Louisville. That was where almost all his business, family, and friends were. During that time, the two men wrote letters to each other giving updates of their progress and looking forward to the time they would meet in Louisville.

William reported that news of a western expedition was creating much interest in Louisville. A number of young men had already asked to go. Captain Clark was a good judge of men. He knew choosing the right men for the party was of the "greatest importance in the success of this vast enterprise." The men he chose made some of the most important contributions to the expedition's success. On August 21, he wrote Lewis that he had promised only four men, who were the "best woodsmen & hunters . . . in this part of the country," that they could go. He "put others off" until Lewis arrived, so they both could decide whether they should go.

Finally, on October 14, Meriwether Lewis arrived at Louisville. The news traveled from Louisville to Lexington, where it was printed in the November 1 edition of the *Kentucky Gazette*. The small notice stated that "Captain Lewis arrived at this port . . . and he and Captain Clark will start in a few days on their expedition to the Westward."

There on the Louisville waterfront, the team of Lewis and Clark, one of the most famous partnerships in history, came together. The two friends must have been very happy to finally join forces. Now they would be working together in their mission to reach the Pacific.

The intended brief stay at The Falls of the Ohio turned into 13 days. No one knows why. On October 15 the boats went through the Falls. In the days that followed, Lewis and Clark made ready to leave. Using the Clark farm at the foot of the Falls as their base, the explorers went back and forth between

> **LOUISVILLE, October 15.**
> Captain Lewis arrived at this port on Friday last. We are informed, that he has brought barges &c. on a new construction, that can be taken in pieces, for the purpose of passing carrying-places; and that he and captain Clark will start in a few days on their expedition to the Westward.

Newspaper report of Lewis's arrival in Louisville, *Kentucky Gazette,* November 1, 1803 (The Filson Historical Society)

Clarksville and Louisville taking care of business and saying their good-byes.

Their most important job was to review the men who wanted go with them. The men who enlisted at The Falls of the Ohio became some of the most important members of the Corps. They became the center around which the rest of the Corps formed. This group is known as the "Nine Young Men from Kentucky." Not all of them were actually from Kentucky. They got that name after the expedition because they were the Corps's first members, the ones who set out from Kentucky with Lewis and Clark in 1803. Clark had seven men waiting for Lewis, and Lewis had two with him. There was no question about some of the men going. In fact, Clark didn't even wait for Lewis's okay before signing up three men. They were Charles Floyd and the brothers Joseph and Reubin Field. After the captains met, John Colter, John Shields, George Gibson, George Shannon, William Bratton, and Nathaniel Pryor were enlisted. Three sergeants served in the Corps. Floyd and Pryor were appointed as two of them, showing the quality of men Clark had chosen from the Louisville area.

But another man must be added to this important group. His name was York. York was William Clark's slave. The two men had grown up together. When William was a boy, York was his servant and playmate. Like his master, York was born in Virginia and had moved to Kentucky with the Clarks. It is believed that York went on trips with William before the expedition. This made him a seasoned traveler. Having him along would make life in camp easier for the captains. But Clark also knew that York could do other things needed on such a trip. He could hunt, scout, and handle a boat. If he had only been a servant, that would have been a luxury the party could not afford. All members of the expedition had to be able to do what was needed and withstand hardship and danger they would face.

After a stay of almost two weeks in Louisville and Clarksville, the explorers set off downriver. The day was overcast and rainy. The date was October 26. William was in Louisville to take care of some business at the courthouse. By that afternoon the captains were ready to leave. Family, friends, and other people would have waved good-bye as the explorers pushed off from Clarksville. Brother Jonathan Clark joined the party for a few miles. He recorded the historic event in his diary, writing, "Capt. Lewis and Capt. Wm. Clark set off on a Western tour." The *Kentucky Gazette* also reported the event. The foundation of the Corps was on its way. It would be three years until their return.

The party made its way down the Ohio. It stopped at West Point, Kentucky. This was where John Shields lived. Although only single men were supposed to go on the expedition, an exception was made for Shields. He was a blacksmith and gunsmith. The captains knew they needed him on the trip to do work involving metal and to fix their guns. He was also a good hunter. Saying good-bye to his wife must have been hard.

There also was a second married man—York. But because he was a slave, he probably didn't have a choice about going. Clark knew he would be useful on the journey and most likely ordered him to go.

Traveling down the Ohio day by day, the Corps made good progress. The captains hoped to get about 200 miles up the Missouri before making winter camp. On November 11 they reached Fort Massac in Illinois. Located across the river from present day Paducah, Kentucky, Massac was a U.S. army post. Here they picked up more men. Some of them would become members of the Corps and others would only help get the boats to Kaskaskia, Illinois. When the party reached the junction of the Ohio and Mississippi Rivers, they planned to go up the Mississippi. That meant they needed extra help getting the boats upstream against the current.

One of the most important members of the expedition joined

at Fort Massac. His name was George Drouillard. He was part French Canadian and part Shawnee Indian and would be an important interpreter, scout, and hunter on the expedition.

After two days at Fort Massac they made the short trip to the junction of the Ohio and Mississippi Rivers. There they looked around for almost a week. An Indian they met wanted to buy Seaman, but Lewis refused. Seaman had already proved his value to the expedition and was part of the team. While they were there, Clark got sick. This was the second time he had become ill. During the expedition almost all the men became sick with various illnesses. The most common ones were diarrhea, boils, colds, and fevers. They also suffered injuries such as cuts, sprains, and snakebite. Lewis treated the men with the medicine he had brought. During the expedition, Lewis and Clark also treated Indians that asked for help.

In late November the keelboat and red pirogue landed at Kaskaskia. Here they recruited more men from the troops stationed at the fort. They also got the white pirogue, the third boat the Corps used to go up the Missouri River.

Lewis went ahead to St. Louis to talk to Spanish officials about going up the Missouri. Clark took the Corps on up the Mississippi to Cahokia, Illinois, near St. Louis. Captain Lewis met the party there and told them that the Spanish refused to let the Corps enter Louisiana Territory. Louisiana was a huge area stretching from the Mississippi River to the Rocky Mountains. The United States had purchased it earlier that year from France but had not yet taken possession of it. The Spanish had owned the territory, but turned it over to France in 1800. Even though

France now owned Louisiana, the Spanish still ruled it, and they refused to let the Americans begin exploring up the Missouri until Louisiana officially belonged to the U.S. That would not be until March 1804. Lewis and Clark would have to wait until spring to start up the river.

This delay probably worked out for the best. The party made its winter camp at the mouth of Wood River on the Mississippi. The French name for the river was Dubois, and this is what they named their camp. Here, across from the mouth of the Missouri River, the men got ready to leave in the spring. Clark was the day-to-day leader of the men. He helped get them ready. Lewis spent most of the winter in St. Louis and Cahokia, getting more information and supplies for the trip.

Some of the Kentuckians and other soldiers got into trouble that winter. There were fights and drunkenness. The Kentucky men were getting used to army life and its rules. Some men refused to follow orders. By the time spring arrived all the men were ready for their great adventure. In March, the Louisiana Territory was turned over to the United States. Lewis and Clark were there to witness the event. By mid-May everything was ready. Spring floods had gone down, the boats were loaded, the men had their orders. The journey west of the Mississippi was about to begin.

3

Up the Missouri

On May 14, 1804, the expedition left Camp Dubois. William Clark recorded the event in his journal. "I set out at 4 O'Clock P.M., in the presence of many of the neighboring inhabitants, and proceeded on under a gentle breeze up the Missouri," he wrote. The West awaited them.

Lewis was not with them yet. He was still in St. Louis taking care of a few final matters. He joined Clark and the rest of the Corps six days later at St. Charles, a small town a short way up the Missouri.

The explorers hunted, fished, and met with Indians. They collected plant and animal samples for President Jefferson. Because he wanted to learn as much as possible about the West, the president told Lewis and Clark to keep daily journals, write reports, and draw maps. To get more information, the captains ordered the sergeants to keep journals and invited the privates to do so if they wished. Seven men, maybe more, kept journals. Six of the seven journals, including those of the two captains, survive in some form today.

Taking the keelboat and pirogues up the Missouri was hard work. The Missouri is a powerful river. In Lewis and Clark's day it was wild and untamed. Traveling against its current day after day wore the men out. Lewis and Clark had hired extra men because of this. If the wind was blowing from the right direction, the men could raise each boat's sail to help them along. Sometimes they moved the boats upstream by rowing, poling, and towing. Towing was especially hard work. A rope was stretched from the boat to men on shore, and the men pulled the boat upriver.

Such hard work made the men very hungry. They had to eat a lot to keep up their energy and strength. Each man ate an average of 8 to 12 pounds of meat a day. This meant a lot of hunting had to be done. Hunting parties were sent out almost every day to kill the game needed to feed this hungry group. The men ate deer, elk, buffalo, bear, rabbit, duck, goose, fish, and other game. This is where the "Nine Young Men from Kentucky" proved their importance. They were the main hunters. To this main diet of meat the explorers added flour, cornmeal, lard, vegetables, fruit, and other food supplies they had brought with them. They also gathered food from the land and from the Indians as they went up the river. In the evening, the men would gather around the camp fires and talk, sing, play music, and even dance if they weren't too tired. They looked forward to their daily ration of whiskey. Tobacco—for smoking and chewing—was a favorite of many of the men.

On August 20, 1804, tragedy struck the Corps of Discovery. Charles Floyd, one of the young Kentuckians, had been sick. It is believed that he had appendicitis and that his appendix burst. In 1804 not even the best doctors could have done anything to help him. By the morning of August 20 he was near death. The captains did what they could to help him. Clark and York were at his side. Floyd knew the end was near. He thought of his family and wanted to say his last good-byes to them. "I am going away," he said to William Clark. "I want you to write me

Pronghorn antelope, one of the animals identified by Lewis and Clark (Drawing by John Woodhouse Audubon. The Filson Historical Society)

a letter." A short time later he died. With great sadness, the party buried this "young man of much merit." Charles Floyd was the only member of the expedition to die on the journey.

As the Corps continued up the Missouri, they entered the Great Plains. They were now traveling through a "sea of grass." No trees could be seen for miles. They saw herds of thousands of buffalo. They saw animals, such as the pronghorn antelope, that were unknown in the United States. They called prairie dogs "barking squirrels." One day the men spent hours trying to flood a prairie dog hole but finally gave up. The men wrote about these unknown animals in their journals and collected samples. Clark drew maps of the Missouri River and the country along it. Lewis collected and described plants. They did their jobs well. Lewis and Clark identified 178 new plants and 122 animals.

The Corps also began meeting more Indians. The captains knew what tribes lived along the Missouri River. These tribes had been in contact with European explorers and traders on the Missouri for many years. Lewis and Clark expected to meet tribes such as the Otoe, Omaha, Yankton Sioux, Teton Sioux, Arikara, Mandan, and Hidatsa. Some tribes were expected to be friendly and others might be hostile. The explorers did not know much about the cultures of these native peoples. Some, like the Tetons, were nomads. They lived in tepees and moved across the prairies. Others, like the Arikara, Mandan, and Hidatsa, lived in permanent lodges made of logs and earth. They farmed the rich bottomland along the river in addition to hunting. The farther west the Corps went the less they knew about the Indians they would meet. The Indians living in the Rocky Mountains and along the Columbia River were more of a mystery than the tribes living along the Missouri River.

The captains followed their orders and tried to meet with as many Indians as possible. At each council (a formal meeting with the Indians), they gave out gifts and made speeches. Their main message was that the Indians were now the children of the "Great White Father" (the president) and that they should obey him. Lewis and Clark were his messengers. Their new "father" wanted his "children" to trade only with Americans. He also invited Indian chiefs to come visit him in Washington so they

Mandan Indians (Karl Bodmer, Joslyn Art Museum, Omaha, Nebraska)

could get to know each other and see the power of the United States.

This message often didn't impress the Indians. Most of the tribes that Lewis and Clark met were still very free. It would be years before the U.S. would be strong enough in the West to make the Indians obey its orders. Until then, the Indians took the Corps's presents and did what they wanted to.

Most meetings with the Indians were friendly, but some were not. One meeting that almost ended up in a fight was with

Teton Sioux Indian (Karl Bodmer, Joslyn Art Museum, Omaha, Nebraska)

the Teton Sioux in September 1804. The Teton Sioux were known as the "bullies of the Missouri." They didn't want anybody going up or down the Missouri without their okay. They wanted to protect their position with other tribes and with traders traveling up and down the river. In exchange for their permission to pass, the Sioux expected presents—lots of presents. Lewis and Clark weren't going to let these "bullies" boss them around. They refused some of the Indians' demands. The Sioux leaders were confused, embarrassed, and angered by this. At one point, the Indians refused to release the pirogue Clark was in. Clark drew his sword and ordered the men to get ready to fight. Guns were aimed and bows were drawn. If a fight had occurred, the expedition could have ended right there. The explorers might have been forced to turn back or even been wiped out. Jefferson was afraid of something like this happening. He had warned Lewis to avoid any fights with Indians, even if it meant turning back.

Clark knew a lot about Indians. He probably knew that they were hoping to scare the white men into giving them more presents. There were women and children by the boat. Clark knew the chiefs did not want them to be hurt. Maybe later they would attack the soldiers but not now. A fight was avoided when the main chief released the boat. Relations improved after this bad start. But by the third day the captains knew they should not stay longer. An incident with two of the boats brought some 200 armed warriors to the river's bank in minutes. Another fight almost occurred when they tried to leave the next day. The Indians grabbed a line of one of the boats. Clark made ready to fire one of the Corps's big guns. The Indians let go of the boat, and the explorers left right away. The group had been lucky to avoid a fight.

Relations with the Arikara Indians were much better. York—Clark's slave from Kentucky—played an important role. The Indians that the Corps met from the Arikara all the way to the Columbia River had never seen a black man before. Because York looked so unusual, the Indians believed he had great spiritual power. The Arikara called him "Big Medicine." They would gather around to look at him. Indian men, women, and

York as created by sculptor Ed Hamilton, Louisville, Kentucky, 2003.

children would touch his skin to see if it was really black and feel his hair to see if it was really like a buffalo's. "All flocked around him & examined him from top to toe," Clark wrote in his journal.

All of a sudden, in the space of months, York went from being a slave with a slave's low position in white society, to being treated with a certain amount of equality on the expedition, to being seen by the Indians as superior to his white companions. York enjoyed this new position. He told the Indians a story about being a wild animal that Clark had caught and tamed. But, he said, he still liked to eat people sometimes. This story, and the looks he would give the Indians, made York "more terrible" than the captains liked. York's strength amazed them.

Lewis and Clark wanted to impress the Indians not scare them. If the Indians were afraid of the explorers, it would be harder to make friends with them. So they told York to stop scaring the Indians. That way they could keep using him to impress the Indians and help the expedition. They also told the other men to behave themselves and do nothing to make the Indians angry.

By late October 1804 the weather was turning cold on the northern Plains. The Corps had reached present-day North Dakota. They knew they could go no farther that fall and must prepare for the winter. Fortunately, their neighbors for the winter were the Mandan Indians. The Mandan were friendly, and everyone got along well. Across the river from a Mandan village, the explorers built a roughly triangular log fort with cabins along two of the inside walls.

The captains used the winter to prepare copies of their journals, reports, and maps. Everyone was excited by what they had seen and done so far. When spring came they would continue upriver. But the keelboat and some of the men would return to St. Louis with the journals, reports, and samples— including a live prairie dog and magpie birds—they had collected. Most of these would be sent to Jefferson and other government officials. Clark sent his rough notes and over 30 souvenirs for family and friends to his brother Jonathan in Louisville.

Lewis and Clark also spent the winter trying to learn more

Mandan Indian village (Drawn by Virginia Smith after a painting by George Caitlin from Smithsonian American Art Museum)

about what lay ahead of them. They talked to the Mandan and the neighboring Hidatsa Indians about the country to the west. This information would be very important. They met a French-Canadian trader named Charbonneau, who lived with the Hidatsa. One of his wives was a young Shoshone Indian woman named Sacagawea. She was about 16 years old. Sacagawea had been captured by the Hidatsa in present-day western Montana about five years earlier. That February she gave birth to her first child. Lewis helped with the delivery. The little boy's father named him Jean Baptiste. But Sacagawea called him Pomp, meaning "first-born" in Shoshone. He was called Pomp or

Pompey by the men. William Clark became very fond of him and years later helped raise him.

Lewis and Clark knew they needed horses from the Shoshone to get across the mountains. It would be good to have this young Indian woman with them. She could speak Shoshone, and they hoped she would be able to recognize landmarks when they got near her homeland in the Rocky Mountains. Also, having a woman in the party was a sign of peace among some tribes, and a woman with a baby was a sign of peace with everybody. A deal was made with Charbonneau. He was hired as an interpreter, and Sacagawea and little Pomp would come too. The captains had made a very good move.

The men may have been living in "most perfect harmony," but they still had to brave the harsh weather conditions. Winters on the northern Plains are very cold. The explorers had thermometers with them. The captains took regular weather readings. During that winter of 1804–1805, they recorded temperatures as cold as -40° F. The Missouri was completely frozen over. A couple of the men suffered minor frostbite while hunting.

The explorers were happy for spring to arrive. By late March the ice had broken up on the river, and the Corps got ready to continue their journey. On April 7, 1805, the captains sent the keelboat back down the Missouri with its precious cargo of expedition journals, reports, and samples. Lewis and Clark and the Corps put into the Missouri with their two pirogues and six dugout canoes. The exploring party numbered 33, including Sacagawea and her baby. The faithful dog Seaman made 34. They were now going where no white men were known to have gone before. William Clark said it well when he wrote his brother Jonathan before setting out, "when I shall have the pleasure of seeing you again is uncertain. . . . The country before me is extensive and unexplored." The Corps of Discovery was stepping off into the unknown.

4

To the Pacific

When Lewis and Clark left Fort Mandan they had only a
general understanding of what lay ahead of them. They had
gotten as much information as possible from the Indians during
the winter. From what they had learned, and from maps and
books they had studied, they knew that the Missouri River
began in the Rocky Mountains and flowed east. They knew
rivers that flowed into the Columbia River began on the other
side of the Rockies and flowed west. The Corps of Discovery
planned to travel these rivers to the Columbia and then follow
the Columbia to the Pacific Ocean.

How hard would it be to cross the mountains? The captains
didn't know. It was believed that the Rockies were only as high
as the Appalachians. If they could find a nice pass—like
Cumberland Gap—to go through, then crossing them wouldn't
be too hard. But what if the Rockies were higher? Either way,
the party knew they had to have horses to cross the mountains.
They would take the boats as far up the river as possible. This
would put them in the area where Sacagawea's people, the
Shoshone, lived. The plan was to trade with them for horses.

Before getting to the mountains, the explorers knew they
had to get around the Great Falls of the Missouri. This was a
major landmark and obstacle on the river. They knew other
Indian tribes lived in the country they would travel through, but
would the Indians be friendly? The explorers also knew they

would see more new kinds of plants and animals. The Indians had warned them about one animal, a fierce bear. The explorers weren't scared. There were bears back home—but not grizzly bears.

To take the place of the keelboat, the men made six dugout canoes. These hollowed-out cottonwood logs joined the red and white pirogues to make up the Corps's little fleet. Day after day the explorers made their way up the Missouri, deeper into unknown country.

One day Seaman was bitten on the leg by a beaver. Everyone was afraid he would die because the bite was so bad, but he got better. That bite was nothing compared to what a bite from a grizzly bear could do to a dog or man. As the Corps traveled farther up the river they met more and more of these dangerous animals. Lewis and Clark often called them "white bears" because of the coloring of their fur. Sometimes, instead of running away, grizzlies would chase them. To be safe, the men often hunted in groups—and still had to be careful. One time it took ten bullets to kill one bear. The explorers grew to respect and fear them. Lewis even confessed in his journal, "I do not like the gentlemen and had rather fight two Indians than one bear."

One night a big buffalo swam the river and charged through their camp. He came within inches of trampling the sleeping men. Seaman heard the beast and came to the rescue. Just as the buffalo neared the captains' tent, Seaman ran at it, barking loudly. The big animal changed course and just missed the tent. Lewis believed his faithful dog had saved them.

The countryside was different from anything they had seen before. The river had eaten through the soft rock to form cliffs on each side. Some of the rocks formed towers and other shapes. Although the country was beautiful, the explorers always had to be on the lookout for bears and Indians. They also had to hunt in order to feed the very hungry members of the party. One day the Corps saw a huge pile of dead, rotting buffalo. Indians had driven them over a cliff. This was one way that the Indians hunted buffalo. They could kill a lot at once and get all the meat, skins, and other parts of the animals that they needed. If there was more than they could use, the rest was left to rot. Lewis noted in his journal that the smell was really bad.

As the Corps made its way westward, thinking the Missouri was on their left, they came to another river on their right side. The Indians hadn't mentioned a second river. It was a big one, and the men weren't sure which one was the Missouri. Should they go up the river to their right or the one to their left? If they took the wrong river and followed it too far before turning around, they might not be able to get to the Pacific that year. If that happened they might have to quit the whole expedition.

Which river should they take? Lewis and Clark were very good about asking the men what they thought when the decision affected the whole group. Even York and Sacagawea got to say what they thought. On this occasion, everybody but Lewis and Clark thought the muddy river coming from the north was the Missouri. It looked just like the river they had been following for over a year. The captains knew the Missouri was coming out of the mountains. They believed the river to the left, with the clearer, swifter water was the one they should take. In order to prove this to the men, they scouted up both rivers. Sure enough, some way up the clear river, the scouting party heard the Great Falls of the Missouri. This was indeed the river they should follow.

Lewis was amazed by the beauty of the falls. There were actually five waterfalls over a ten-mile stretch of the river. Lewis described them in his journal: the roar the water made as it went over the falls and beat upon rocks, the foamy white color of the water, the spray rising in the air, a rainbow at the bottom of one of the falls. He wrote that words to properly describe how "grand" and "beautiful" they were failed him.

The falls may have been beautiful, but everyone knew it was going to be very hard work to get around them. It took two weeks to get the dugout canoes around the falls. The pirogues were too big, and they were hidden along the river below the falls. The men made crude carts from trees to move the boats. It was very hard work. The land was rough. There were hardly any trees. Terrible storms, including a hail storm, pounded them. The hail was so bad that it knocked the men down and gave them cuts and bruises. Clark, Sacagawea, her husband, and her little baby got caught in this storm and took cover in a ravine. All of a sudden a flood swept through the ravine. Clark got them out just in time. York was very worried about them and braved the storm looking for them. He arrived just as they climbed out.

Finally, a month after arriving at the Great Falls, the boats had been taken around them, and the explorers had rested up. They were ready to continue their journey.

As the explorers continued upriver, they left the Great Plains behind and entered the foothills of the Rocky Mountains. They arrived at the Three Forks, where three rivers come together to form the Missouri. This was country that Sacagawea remembered from her childhood. She had been captured in this area. The captains decided which of the rivers they should follow. This time everyone trusted them to pick the right one, and they kept going.

The Corps of Discovery followed the Jefferson River first and then the Beaverhead River deeper into the mountains. They looked for Shoshone Indians. Finally, in the middle of August, Lewis met some. He was scouting ahead of the group with a few men, and they surprised some women picking berries. Lewis told them he was friendly and came in peace. To try to prove it he gave them presents. The women's fear turned to joy, and they led the explorers toward their village.

The little party had gone about two miles when about 60 warriors rode out to meet them. The Indian women showed the chief the presents Lewis had given them. Everybody was happy, and the explorers were hugged over and over again. Lewis told the chief and warriors he came in peace and friendship. He also told them that he was traveling with a larger group of white men, a black man, wonderful trade goods, and a Shoshone woman who had once lived in that country. The Indians were curious to see these wonders. They agreed to go with Lewis and his small scouting party back to the river where they could see these things for themselves.

So away they went. The group reached the river and waited for Clark and the main party to appear. The Indians worried a little bit that this might be a trick to attack them, but Clark soon came into view with the boats. The Shoshone then saw the wonders Lewis had promised them—a black man, a Shoshone woman, fine trade goods, and even Seaman, who also amazed the Indians.

The Shoshone chief and the captains began to talk. Lewis and Clark wanted to tell the chief more about their mission and their need for horses to get across the mountains. Good communication was very important, and Sacagawea was asked to interpret. She had just begun when she suddenly cried out and threw her arms around the chief. He was her brother. What good luck; with this connection, the Indians and explorers became very friendly. The Corps got the horses they needed, and the Shoshone got trade goods and promises of more when other Americans visited them in the future.

Lewis and Clark knew by now that getting across the mountains was going to be hard. There was no one easy place to march through them. Although it was still August, the nights were cold. They had to get across quickly and soon. An Indian went with the party to help guide them. Even with his help they sometimes lost their way. They had to go up and down mountainsides. The trail was nothing more than animal paths. The explorers were cold, wet, and very hungry—so hungry that they ate some of their horses. The snow was sometimes six to

Sacagawea and baby Pomp (Drawn by Virginia Smith)

eight inches deep. William Clark wrote in his journal in the middle of September that he was as wet, cold, and miserable as he had ever been in his life. Of the more than eight thousand miles the Corps traveled, they believed this was the worst part of the entire trip.

But good luck continued with Lewis and Clark. Finally, they got through the mountains. On the other side they met the Nez Perce Indians who lived along the Clearwater River. This river would lead to the Snake River, and that waterway to the Columbia. The Nez Perce were friendly and fed the explorers fish and roots. They were so hungry they ate too much, and most of the men got sick. After everyone got better, the Nez

Perce showed them an easier way to make dugout canoes using fire. The Corps made five canoes and headed for the Pacific.

It was much easier and faster going with the river current instead of against it. But the explorers still had to be careful. They were traveling on wild and dangerous rivers. Sometimes they rode their canoes through rapids, and other times they had to unload everything and carry it and the boats around rapids and waterfalls.

As they had traveled down the Columbia, they met more Indians the closer they got to the Pacific. These Indians were different from Indians the explorers had met before. They looked different and their cultures were different. Many Indians were camped along the river catching fish for their winter food supply. The captains noted in their journals that the smell of all the dead and rotting fish was awful. The Indians on the lower Columbia had seen white men and even black men before. The few trade goods that Lewis and Clark had left were nothing special to them. These Indians had been trading for years with ships sailing along the Pacific coast. Some had even picked up a little English, including swear words.

As the explorers got close to the ocean, the Columbia got so wide that they thought they'd reached the Pacific. Clark wrote, "Ocean in View, O! The joy!" But it was more than a week before they actually reached the Pacific. They were stopped just short of their goal by a terrible storm. For almost a week they clung to the shore and were pounded by rain, wind, and waves. When the storm passed, they finally reached the ocean. There was indeed great joy. This was the goal they had worked so long and hard to reach. The Corps of Discovery had made Thomas Jefferson's dream come true.

It was the middle of November by now, and the captains knew they couldn't get back over the mountains before the snow was too deep to travel through. They would have to build a fort for the winter near the Pacific. Instead of having a good winter as they did among the Mandan Indians, the Corps looked forward to a wet, miserable one among Indians they didn't like very much.

Knowing they were all in this together, the captains did as they had before when the opinion of the whole group was important. They asked everyone, including York and Sacagawea, where they wanted to spend the winter. The majority wanted to stay on the south side of the Columbia. Lewis and Clark agreed. They crossed to the south side and built Fort Clatsop (named after the local Indian tribe). It was here that they spent a very wet, chilly, and miserable winter. It rained a lot. There was almost no sunshine. Their food wasn't very good. Since reaching the Columbia, dogs had become a regular part of their diet. Most of the men liked the meat, but Clark didn't. A small party of men made salt from ocean water to help season and preserve their food. Some of the salt makers were from Kentucky and may have worked in salt works back home. One of the most memorable events of the winter was seeing a whale that had washed up on the beach. Everyone looked forward to spring when they could start for home.

Fort Clatsop replica (Lewis and Clark Trail Heritage Foundation, Great Falls, Montana)

5

Homeward Bound

The explorers were so eager to start for home that they left Fort Clatsop a month too early. In late March 1806 they left their winter home and started up the Columbia. They continued to keep journals, draw maps, and collect samples, but they also tried to travel as fast as possible.

As the Corps moved eastward along the Columbia, they met many Indians. Most of the meetings were friendly, but some were not. The explorers almost got into a fight with some Indians who stole Seaman. Lewis gave orders to shoot the thieves if necessary, but the men rescued the dog without violence. There seemed to be regular cases of items being stolen or a fight almost taking place. The explorers disliked the local Indians so much that they didn't want to leave anything behind for them to use. When they were done with their boats, Lewis ordered them burned rather than left for the Indians.

The Corps continued eastward toward the mountains. They reunited with the Nez Perce on the west side of the Rockies. The explorers believed they were again among friends. It was a good thing they felt that way. In their eagerness to leave their winter camp, they had reached the mountains too soon. The snow was still so deep in the Bitterroots that the Corps spent more than a month with the Nez Perce. They passed the time pleasantly, visiting and playing games. The captains kept busy doctoring sick Indians. The Nez Perce remembered Lewis and

Clark so fondly that they remained friends with the U.S. until the 1870s, when they fought to try to keep their homeland.

Finally, the snow melted enough to allow the Corps to cross the mountains. Three Nez Perce guides took the party across the trail. On the last day of June they reached the east side of the mountains.

The captains were now faced with a hard decision. Should they stay together or should they split up for a while in order to explore more country? They had earlier made a plan that called for Lewis to take nine men directly east to the Great Falls of the Missouri. Once there, he planned to take six of the men north toward Canada. Clark, meanwhile, would retrace part of their route from the year before and get the canoes they left along the Beaverhead River. His group would float downstream to the Three Forks of the Missouri (where three rivers form the Missouri). From the Three Forks, a party would take boats to the Great Falls to join Lewis. Clark would take the rest overland to the Yellowstone River and explore down it.

Not much happened to Clark and his party. Indians stole all their horses, so everyone, instead of just part of the group, floated down the Yellowstone. It was along the Yellowstone that William Clark left behind evidence of the Lewis and Clark Expedition's passing through the American West. In late July, the party came to a large rock formation along the river. Clark named it Pompey's Pillar, in honor of Sacagawea's little boy, of whom he was very fond. On it Clark carved his name and date.

Meanwhile, a lot was happening to Lewis and his party. They reached the Great Falls without much trouble. Indians had stolen some of their horses. This caused Lewis to take only three men (Drouillard and the Field brothers) on his scouting trip to the north. The result was almost a disaster. While scouting along the Two Medicine River, they met a band of eight Blackfeet Indians. That night the Indians camped with them. At dawn the next day, the Blackfeet tried to steal the explorers' guns and horses. Lewis and his men had no choice but to fight. They could not be left on foot without guns so far away from the others. In the fight that followed, two Indians were killed. Lewis and his men kept their guns and horses. They quickly traveled south and met up with the rest of the party on the Missouri.

This fight with the Blackfeet was the only actual bloodshed between the Corps and American Indians during the whole expedition. Of the thousands of encounters that took place between the explorers and native peoples, this was the only one that ended in violence. This is a tribute to the captains and their men and the way they interacted with the Indians. It is also a tribute to the Indians. Without their goodwill toward this small band of explorers, Lewis and Clark never would have achieved their mission for President Jefferson. They never even would have gotten very far up the Missouri River.

Lewis's adventures weren't over yet. Just one day before rejoining Clark and his party, Lewis went hunting. The captain chose a bad hunting partner. Pierre Cruzatte was blind in one eye and couldn't see very well out of the other. He mistook his leader for an elk (all the men wore animal skin clothes by now) and shot him in the backside. The rifle ball passed through the left buttock and creased the right one. Fortunately, no bone or artery was hit. But Lewis spent a painful three weeks, often lying face down in a boat, recovering from his wound. By the end of the fourth week, Clark wrote in his journal, "My worthy friend Capt. Lewis has entirely recovered."

While Lewis was recovering from his wound, the Corps reached the Mandan and Hidatsa villages. Here they parted with Charbonneau, Sacagawea, and little Pomp. Clark was sorry to leave them behind. Just a few days after leaving them, he wrote Charbonneau a letter offering to take the little boy home and "educate him and treat him as my own child." Clark also wrote that he was sorry that they could not reward Sacagawea for all the help she had given them. He offered to help Charbonneau in any way he could. The captain's offer was turned down for the time being, but eventually Clark did help raise Pomp, and he gave Charbonneau a job.

Another parting that took place at the villages was with John Colter. The blue-eyed Kentuckian had fallen in love with the West. When the Corps met two Americans going to the mountains to trap beaver, Colter got Lewis and Clark's permission to go with them. Before finally returning down the Missouri River four years later, John Colter had many adventures and close calls with death.

After leaving the Arikara villages, near the present North and South Dakota state line, the explorers headed for home as quickly as possible. The Missouri's current was now pushing the Corps along instead of holding them back as it did when they went up the river in 1804 and 1805. Making 10 or 12 miles a day upstream was considered good progress. Now, traveling with the river current, the Corps sometimes traveled as many as 70 miles in a day. One problem they faced was the wind. It blew so hard against them some days that they had trouble moving. This was nothing new. The wind was often a problem for the explorers on the expedition. Sometimes they rowed, poled, and paddled just to keep from being blown backward by the wind.

The closer the explorers got to St. Louis, the more eager they were to keep moving. The men still had to eat, but some days they ate only one meal and didn't stop to rest. The Teton Sioux tried to get the Corps to stop, but Clark ignored them. He remembered their tense meeting with these Indians two years ago. The last thing Clark wanted now was a fight when they were so close to completing the expedition.

By early September, the Corps began meeting traders coming up the river. From these men, the explorers got news of home. They learned that President Jefferson had been elected to a second term, and there was talk of war with England. They stopped to visit the grave of Charles Floyd and then "proceeded on." Just nine days from reaching St. Louis, the explorers met traders who gave them biscuits, pork, and whiskey. The whiskey was especially welcome. The men were happy and sang songs late into the night.

On September 20 the Corps saw their first town in over two years. As they passed it and other towns along the river, the people lined the banks and cheered. The explorers cheered too and fired off their guns in salute. On September 23, at about noon the Corps of Discovery arrived in St. Louis. They were greeted as returning heroes. Most people thought they had died. There had been reports in newspapers that Indians had killed them. And here they were.

Lewis and Clark knew they had to get word out to the country that they had made it back. The best way to do that was to write a letter to William's brother Jonathan in Louisville. A letter from Lewis all the way to Jefferson in Washington would take much longer. The two captains sat down that night and worked on the letter. It was a summary of the expedition since the Corps left Fort Mandan in April 1805. They sent it to Jonathan, and Jonathan sent it to a Frankfort newspaper. But word of the expedition's return raced ahead of the captains' letter. On October 2, 1806, the Frankfort *Palladium* newspaper published the first report of the Corps's return. Then, a week later, it published William's letter. Other papers printed these two reports, and within a month, the whole country knew that the Lewis and Clark Expedition had successfully returned from the Pacific Ocean.

But there was more still to do. Lewis and Clark discharged the men and got ready to head east—and home. With them went some expedition members and two parties of Indians, one all the way from the Mandans. On November 5, 1806, they reached Louisville. It had been just over three years since they pushed off from the Falls of the Ohio on their journey. The day they got back, William went shopping on Main Street. On November 8, the captains were the guests of honor at a Clark family celebration at Locust Grove, the home of William's sister Lucy Croghan. Locust Grove is best known as the last home of George Rogers Clark. But it is also a very important Lewis and

Newspaper report of Lewis and Clark return, *The Palladium,* October 9, 1806 (The Filson Historical Society)

Clark site. The historic home is the only known existing Lewis and Clark building west of the Appalachians.

A few days after this celebration, Lewis left for Washington. The Indians and other men went with him. At Frankfort the group split up. Some of the men went through Lexington and eastward on to Washington. Lewis, who had the Mandan Indians with him, took the famous Wilderness Road through Kentucky to the Cumberland Gap. After visiting his mother in Charlottesville, Virginia, he went on to Washington and a reunion with President Jefferson.

In mid-December William Clark and York left Louisville for Washington. They took the Wilderness Road to Danville where William visited some of his nephews at school. From there they went through the Cumberland Gap and on to Fincastle, Virginia, to visit a special young lady. William had named the Judith River in present Montana in her honor. Now he visited her on his way to Washington with an "object in view." That object was marriage.

By mid-January Lewis and Clark reunited in Washington. There they were honored as returning heroes. The leaders of the United States knew what these brave men and their followers had done for their country. They were rewarded with extra pay and land grants. Lewis and Clark also were given important government jobs. Thomas Jefferson did whatever he could to help them. After all, these two men had made his long-time dream of exploring the West come true.

Meriwether Lewis and William Clark had led the most famous exploring venture in American history. They also formed one of the most famous and successful partnerships in history. The future seemed bright.

6

Life after the Expedition

The Lewis and Clark Expedition had been the biggest event in the lives of its members. Most of the explorers were still fairly young, in their 20s and 30s. Sacagawea wasn't even 20 years old yet. And little Jean Baptiste wasn't even two. What did the future hold for the members of the Corps of Discovery? Did it hold happiness and long lives or did it hold disappointment, suffering, and early death?

The lives of the Nine Young Men from Kentucky would takes both paths. Charles Floyd, of course, never came home. He lay buried on a hill overlooking the Missouri River, the only member of the Corps to die on the expedition.

The Field brothers were two of Lewis and Clark's best men. After the expedition, Lewis described the brothers as "two of the most active and enterprising young men who accompanied us," who had "engaged in all the most dangerous and difficult scenes of the voyage." Perhaps Joseph Field's luck ran out. He was the first to die after the Corps's return. It isn't known how, where, and exactly when he died. He was dead by October 1807. Years later, William Clark reported that Joseph had been killed. It is possible that he was killed by Indians. His brother Reubin's fate was happier. After the expedition he married and settled on a farm in Jefferson County. He died in late 1822 or early 1823.

George Gibson married a Louisville woman and briefly

lived in the area. While they were moving to St. Louis, he died on the Mississippi River in January 1809. John Shields was reunited with his wife upon his return home. They moved across the Ohio River to southern Indiana. He died in December 1809. William Bratton married a Kentucky woman, served in the War of 1812, and moved to Waynetown, Indiana, in 1822. There he served as a justice of the peace and as a school superintendent and died in 1841.

George Shannon became the best-educated member of the Corps of Discovery. He lost a leg in an 1807 Indian fight, went to Transylvania University in Lexington, and helped to write the official expedition history. He became a lawyer, politician, and judge. He married a woman from Lexington in 1813 and moved to Missouri about 1828. There he continued the practice of law and was active in politics. He dropped dead in the courtroom while trying a murder case in 1836.

Nathaniel Pryor also had some close calls with Indians. The Kentuckian stayed in the army after the expedition and became an officer. He got out of the army and worked as an Indian trader and in the lead furnace business on the Mississippi. An Indian attack destroyed that business, and he rejoined the army. Pryor rose to the rank of captain and fought at the Battle of New Orleans in January 1815. He later returned to the Indian trade, settled in present-day Oklahoma, and married an Indian woman. He died in 1831.

The last of the Nine Young Men became the most famous. John Colter became the first "mountain man" and had many adventures in the West. He was the first white man to see the wonders of the geysers and hot springs of what would become Yellowstone National Park. He had run-ins with Indians. The most famous run-in was in 1808 when the Blackfeet captured him. They stripped him naked and told him to start running. The Indians let him get a head start and then chased after him, thinking they would catch him. But they had not counted on Colter's running ability. He outran all but one Indian. Just as that warrior was ready to catch him, Colter turned around, grabbed the Indian's spear and killed him. Colter then jumped in the river and hid in a beaver's den. The other Indians were very angry at this turn of events. They looked for Colter but couldn't find him. When it was safe, Colter began walking to a fort over 200 miles away—and made it. In 1810 after another close call, he decided his luck was used up. He settled in Missouri, married, and died in 1812 or 1813.

Captain Lewis described George Drouillard after the expedition as a "man of much merit," whose skills as an interpreter, hunter, and woodsman were important to the expedition's success. Lewis also noted, as he had with the Field brothers, that he had taken part in "all the most dangerous and trying scenes of the voyage." Their close call with the Blackfeet in July 1806 no doubt made Drouillard and the Field brothers special to him. Drouillard returned to the mountains, like Colter and other expedition veterans, to trap beaver. A fortune could be made in beaver furs if you were lucky. But luck only holds for so long, and even the best mountain man could meet up with bad luck. George survived his fight with the Blackfeet in 1806, but he didn't survive his 1810 fight with them. While checking his traps along the Jefferson River, he was attacked by a party of Blackfeet. After putting up a hard fight, he was killed and hacked into pieces.

Other members of the expedition met fates similar to these men. Some were killed by Indians, and others died of natural causes. The fate of some remains unknown. Patrick Gass and Alexander H. Willard lived long enough to have their photographs taken. Gass was the last living member of the Corps. He lived to be 98 years old and died in 1870.

On the expedition, York had enjoyed a degree of equality and freedom he never had before. What was his fate? There is a story that York returned to the Rocky Mountains where he lived a happy life among the Crow Indians. It is much more likely that he died of disease in Tennessee. After the expedition, York and his master, William Clark, had a falling out. Clark moved to St. Louis in 1808 and took York with him. York's wife was owned by someone else and stayed in Louisville. York wanted to stay in Louisville so he could be near his wife. Clark at first refused, but York made his unhappiness so well known that Clark eventually changed his mind. He got so angry with York that he threatened to sell him, and on one occasion he beat him. From 1809 to 1816 York worked in Louisville. One of his major jobs was driving a wagon around town making deliveries. At least nine years after his return from the Pacific, York was still a slave. Sometime between 1816 and 1832, William Clark freed him and set him up in a freight hauling business in Kentucky and Tennessee. In 1832 Clark reported that York had lost the business and died in Tennessee while trying to return to him in St. Louis. This most likely was York's fate. The first African American to cross the United States from coast to coast, and one of the most famous black Americans in our nation's early history, probably lies in an unmarked pauper's grave.

What about the expedition's only woman and child? Sacagawea only lived six years after her journey to the Pacific. In December 1812, not long after having her second child, she died at Fort Manuel on the Missouri River. She was about 24 years old. Her story, however, like York's, has another ending. An old Indian woman living in Wyoming in the 1880s claimed she was Sacagawea. Some believe this to be true. But the best evidence, including court documents and a statement by William Clark, confirm that she died in 1812.

Sacagawea's baby "Pomp," little Jean Baptiste, lived an interesting life. In 1806, Clark offered to take the boy and raise him as his own. Following Sacagawea's death, Clark adopted him and his little sister. In 1823 Pomp met a German prince traveling in the West and went back to Europe with him. Six years later he returned to the United States and the West. He was a mountain man, a trader, and a guide for government explorers. He lived in California for some years, and died in 1866 in Oregon while on his way to the Montana gold mines.

And what of the captains? The lives of these famous partners were very different after the expedition. William Clark worked for the government for the rest of his life. He served as a general in the militia, the head Indian agent, and governor of Missouri Territory. Clark tried to do the best job he could for the government. He also tried to treat the Indians as fairly as possible and protect them from the rush of settlers moving west. William married twice, in 1808 and 1821. He outlived both his wives and three of his seven children. William Clark died in St. Louis in 1838 at the age of 68.

Meriwether Lewis's death came only three years after the expedition. While Clark's life was long and full, Lewis's was short and sad. His reward as co-leader of the expedition was to be named governor of the Louisiana Territory. But Lewis wasn't a politician. He had political enemies who worked against him. He wanted to get married but failed to find a bride. He had financial troubles. Jefferson had told him to write the expedition history, but he hadn't done it. His health became a problem. He began drinking too much. The final blow came when the government refused to pay some of his bills. There were rumors of dishonesty and corruption.

In this state of mind, on the verge of a breakdown—physical and mental—Meriwether Lewis left for Washington in the late summer of 1809 to settle his problems. He also took the expedition journals with him to go to Philadelphia and work on the book. Lewis never got there. While sailing down the Mississippi River from St. Louis, he suffered a breakdown and twice tried to kill himself. When the boat reached an army post at present-day Memphis, Tennessee, the post commander confined him for about two weeks until he seemed to get better. Lewis then headed east with a small party. But his problems soon returned.

On the night of October 10, 1809, at a lonely inn on the Natchez Trace about 80 miles southwest of Nashville, Meriwether Lewis took out his pistols, loaded them, and shot himself once in the head and once in the body. In his pain and madness, he was reported to have even taken his razor and cut himself many times. The famous explorer lingered through the night and died early on the morning of October 11. Among Meriwether Lewis's last reported words were, "I have done the deed," and "it is so hard to die."

But did Lewis commit suicide? About 30 years later a rumor began that he was actually murdered. The reasons varied from political enemies getting rid of him to robbery. The murder theory has its supporters today, but most people believe, as everyone in 1809 believed—including William Clark and Thomas Jefferson—that Lewis killed himself. Thus ended the life of one of America's greatest explorers.

The members of the Corps of Discovery are long dead, but they live on today. Books, magazines, movies, television, radio, exhibits, paintings, posters, and more all remember these famous Americans. What they achieved for the United States some 200 years ago was awesome, and we are still studying, learning from, and enjoying their adventures today.

About the Author

James J. Holmberg is the curator of special collections at The Filson Historical Society in Louisville, Kentucky, where he has worked for over 20 years. He has degrees in history from the University of Louisville.

He is the editor of *Dear Brother: Letters of William Clark to Jonathan Clark* and wrote the epilogue for the revised edition of *In Search of York: The Slave Who Went to the Pacific with Lewis and Clark*. He writes and lectures on the Lewis and Clark Expedition. His articles frequently appear in the national Lewis and Clark magazine, *We Proceeded On*. Mr. Holmberg has also written entries for *The Kentucky Encyclopedia*, *The Encyclopedia of Louisville*, and the *Dictionary of Virginia Biography*. He is a member of the Kentucky Humanities Council's Speakers Bureau.

Mr. Holmberg is married and has three children. His wife Ruthe Pfisterer Holmberg works in higher education and college admissions. They live in Louisville.